Keys For Moms

Kasia Rachfall MNLP, MATP, CPC

Keys For Moms

Enough is Enough!
Simple Strategies for Identifying and
Silencing the Lies You've Been
Telling Yourself

Fresh Perspective Family – A Leading Neuro
Dynamics Company

Leading Neuro Dynamics Press

Editor: Rosemary Sneeringer
Format: Margaret Florczak
Cover Design: Evolution Graphic Design
Cover Photo: Bryan Rachfall

ISBN 978-0-9868559-0-0

Published by Leading Neuro Dynamics Press

This book is meant to educate and inspire through the many stories and experiences of the author. The author, editor, and publisher of this publication are not responsible for the result of any action taken on the basis of information in this work, nor for any errors or omissions. The ideas, procedures, and suggestions described in this book are not intended as a substitute for consulting with your physician or mental health professional. If other expert assistance is required, the services of a competent professional should be sought. All stories and clients mentioned in this book are compilations for the author's experiences, gathered during the author's personal and professional practice.

Library and Archives Canada Cataloguing in Publication

Rachfall, Kasia, 1978-
      Keys for moms : enough is enough! : simple strategies for identifying and silencing the lies you've been telling yourself / Kasia Rachfall.

Includes bibliographical references.
ISBN 978-0-9868559-0-0

      1. Mothers--Attitudes. 2. Mothers--Psychology. 3. Self-realization in women. I. Title.

HQ759.R235 2011   646.70085'2   C2011-900929-3

With all my love for Braeden and Kaitlyn –
they handed me the keys to my life and for Bryan –
who stood by me while I learned to use them.

Contents

PART I

Keys For Moms

My Story

We all have a journey to make in this life, and it is up to us what road we will take. My own road was suffering and retelling my old story over and over. It never occurred to me that I could choose to learn and grow from my story. I was stuck, but I found ways to move forward, and now that I have been on both sides of the old story, I prefer growing over suffering.

My transformation happened years ago at Christmastime. A storm was raging outside, not unusual for Vancouver in the winter. I was sitting on the floor of my living room sobbing uncontrollably while my husband slept, exhausted from working 20-hour days. My babies, too, were sleeping peacefully, despite my endless yelling throughout the day.

My post-partum depression was raging, and my world was collapsing. Over and over again, the thoughts circled: I'm worthless; I'm a horrible mother; I don't deserve to live.

3

That was my experience in 2004 after my daughter was born. I felt wretched and alone, and I really did not think I was strong enough to carry on one more day. We were broke, I was hormonal, stressed, and depressed. I saw no way out. I admit that I contemplated suicide.

In that dark moment, I felt a tiny sliver of curiosity and tenacity. It was so small that I can't even call it a light. It was more of a fleeting feeling that flickered like a distant candle somewhere in a dark forest. Yet I knew unmistakably it was there – and this feeling wanted acknowledgement.

Somewhere deep inside, at some level, I wanted better circumstances in my life. And I knew I deserved better!

Other people I had met were happy and successful in their lives – didn't I deserve that too?

I didn't know how I would dig myself out of my hole, but the important part was that I knew in that moment I wasn't going to commit suicide. I would find a way.

***

Three weeks later, for my birthday, my mom gave me a book called *The Power Of Intention* by Dr. Wayne Dyer. Although I didn't understand most of the concepts, I felt this book was my ladder out of that hole! I began reading, listening, studying and learning everything I could about the mind and how we create our lives. I continue to do this even today because there is so much to know*!* *I kept a list of everything that worked and threw out everything that didn't. That dark moment in my life was a*

4

turning point, and I decided to devote the rest of my professional career to helping others crawl out of their own dark holes.

***

Fast-forward a few years and my story has completely changed. I am fulfilled. I have two amazingly strong and beautifully confident, loving children, and a husband who is strong and supportive. I am living my life's dream and purpose. I am empowering other women and moms to help themselves find their own power.

This book is the culmination of years of hard work and experience. I uncovered my own inner strength and balance. I learned what it means to have personal excellence and meaningful internal and external communication. I have developed my personal empowerment and self-esteem. I feel happy and I am kinder to myself and to others.

In my profession and in my life, I have been told that I give too much away. Yet I believe my knowledge is only of value if I share it with others. That's why I wrote this book. *Because I can't personally work with every woman and mother out there who wants to help herself, I have compiled simple tools so you can change your own story and make your dreams a reality.*

Don't you owe it to yourself to do this? Once and for all, take charge of your life and *drive it forward* instead of being driven.

What Do Some Women Know That You Don't?

Do you ever wonder why some women are living the lives of their dreams? They find the time to handle their responsibilities *and* their hobbies with a huge smile on their face. Women just like YOU: working moms who have kids, obligations and careers.

What do they know that you don't? What helps them float through each day, making it look so easy? What allows them to smile through stressful times instead of tearing their hair out or getting depressed? What secret keys do they hold?

It's time to reveal to you the keys to living a life that YOU control and not a life that controls YOU. This secret key is simple. It's so simple that you may laugh at it and say to yourself, "I know that already!"

Yes, you know it already. BUT the question is: are you *living* it? Are you experiencing the results you want from applying this knowledge in your life? If not, then it is time to use the wisdom and step-by-step program in this book. All knowledge becomes "shelf help" unless you implement it!

Ready? Here it is: *YOU hold the keys to living an empowered life in YOUR hands. When you take 100% responsibility for your choices, your actions and your inactions, your life will change immediately. You'll recognize the excuses and reasons you have for staying in your comfort zone and suffering through your current story, and your story will change!* You are the creator of your reality. Dr Wayne Dyer says that when you change the way you look at things, the things you look at change. It's true. *You will see immediate results when you use this book because your mindset will shift.*

But first, you must take inventory of where you are now and what you think and believe about yourself. Come clean -- are you living the life of your dreams? No?

Have you ever asked yourself *why not?* What answers came to you? Did you act on any of those? Why not? What stopped you? What excuses did you give yourself? How did you convince yourself to stay in the same place in your life?

Let's explore the possible answers and what you can do to stop convincing yourself to stay stagnant and instead start moving toward the life you want and know you deserve to live.

Are You Squeezing 36 Hours Worth of "Stuff" Into A 24-Hour Day?

Life in the 21st century is HECTIC! With today's technology, we're constantly connected to all sorts of input and there's little down time. Now that you're a mom, it seems that there's even less time than ever before!

You're busy carpooling, squeezing in laundry, cooking nutritious meals, packing lunches, helping with housework, pitching in with yard work and . . . sleeping. If you do have energy, you're thinking about going to the gym, doing yoga or having a night out with the girls.

You're so busy doing things for your family that I'm willing to bet that YOU come last! At the same time you're probably saying to yourself, "It's my responsibility to do these things! I'm the mom!"

Of course you are. And you're also much more than that! Dr. Matthew James has a great saying: "Whatever you think you are, you're more than that!" Take a moment to think about all those things you are that you don't allow yourself to be because you've put yourself in a box: "mom," "wife," "employee." Boxes and roles do not leave much room for self love, self- expression, pursuing passions and dreams, taking care of yourself and focusing on your own happiness. Do you get so run down trying to fulfill the roles that you don't take time for yourself, and then complain about it to your girlfriends or husband?

Deep down, you know if you let go of the guilt about taking care of yourself and you stopped feeling afraid of changing things that aren't working in your life, you would feel happier, more fulfilled, and less resentful of all those responsibilities you have taken on.

Please know that it's okay to feel this way! There is nothing wrong with you wanting to break out of the mold you're in right now, because you are here for a purpose, and if you're not living that purpose, you can't really be happy deep down to your soul because you're denying your soul its self-expression.

What Are The True Costs of This Fast-Paced Life You're Living?

Do you sometimes feel that life is passing you by and that you're not getting to do what you've always wanted to do? Sure, you wanted to get married, have kids, own a house and have a career. But what other dreams and goals slipped away as you've assumed these responsibilities? Did you want to paint, write, dance or travel? Where have your dreams gone?

What Calling Have You Put Aside To Be a Mom, a Wife and a Professional?

You worry that the pace of life is affecting your relationships with your children. You squeeze in quality time between sports and cooking dinner. Even then your mind is filled with things you have yet to do, and you're trying to remember them all. You worry about what your children are learning because you know that you are their greatest role model. You wonder how you will raise well-adjusted and self-actualized adults when you're constantly busy *doing* all the time.

You worry whether your kids have good self-esteem and if they're doing well in school. You worry about them having the confidence to say no to drugs and other undesirable behaviors. You worry, worry, worry! How much energy are you investing in your worries -- energy that could be freed up to use more productively.

9

As a mother, you are one of the biggest role models in your children's lives. What kind of example do you set for your children if you are not taking care of yourself?

Do you get angry easily? Do you yell a lot? Do your children listen to you?

When you listen to your children do you hear what they are saying, or do your thoughts race to your to-do list. Do your children listen? Or do you have to repeat yourself several times before they respond? Teaching your children how to listen requires that *you* listen to *them* first. By not being mindful with your children, you're not setting a good example for them to be fully present and responsive when they are with you or other people.

Do you constantly imagine what others are thinking about you as you go about your day? Do you feel like a zombie chained to your tight schedule? ***Do you feel you've lost yourself somewhere along the way and you're taking care of everything and everyone else except you? You tell yourself "someday" you will be able to find the time to enjoy your hobbies and work on your personal growth. For now, you're going through the motions day after day -- and the years slip by.***

You are the cornerstone of your family – that's what moms are. You're the go-to person for everything. Do you feel like a cornerstone or like a piece of duct tape holding everything together?

You have these amazing abilities to know where things are, where to find lost keys, shoes, stuffed animals, to throw together a nutritious meal within a few minutes, to zip around from activity to activity and seemingly be in two places at once. You're a superhero!

So Why Do You Feel Like You've Lost Yourself?

You have many excuses as to why you don't take care of yourself. No time, no money, this appointment or that sports practice or after-school activity. You feel selfish if you want some time to yourself, but you feel no one else can do the job you do.

Where do these excuses come from? Why do moms keep using them? Is it to take the focus off of yourself and the really deep needs and desires you carry? Remember, if you do what you've always done, you'll get what you've always gotten. What reward are you getting from using these excuses? There is always a payoff for our behaviors or we wouldn't do them.

Perhaps you just don't know what you want to do in your life. You have this awareness growing deep inside, but you can't put a finger on it. You know that if you just figured it out, you would know what to do next. Your path would clear itself before you and you wouldn't be afraid of just "going for it."

My Intention For You

Just because this is your life now doesn't mean it has to be that way forever. In fact, you have the power to change it today. ***Right now.*** You just have to choose to change and give yourself permission. This is *very* important. You can only change what you are 100% committed to changing. And you have to want to do it for yourself. ***If you want to change for someone else, it won't work.*** This is not being selfish -- this is a fact: the more energy you have, the more fulfilled you are, the better your family and everything else in your life will fare.

You have this awareness that your life is not your own - if you want to reclaim it and make it your own you must know your reasons for doing so. It will take practice and perseverance, but it will be worth it for you. You'll see results right away if you commit to the process.

What Does Kasia Know?

As you read earlier, I was where you are not too long ago. I was on the brink of taking a drastic measure because I felt so depressed and helpless. I was being pulled in so many directions that I didn't know who I was anymore. In the midst of postpartum depression and deep financial troubles, I wanted to end the struggle. I knew there had to be a better way to live but I didn't know where to start.

I had always wondered why some people seemed to have it so easy and why things worked for them. I had a vague curiosity inside me that grew into a desire to discover their secret. I needed to know what they knew. *My discovery shocked me because of its simplicity.*

I've lived the research, I've read, listened to, and watched hours of information on changing my life. I've distilled the path to change and simplified it for you. In your time-squeezed world, I know you don't have the time to read book after self-help book. My knowledge and research are based on the work of scientists, spiritual masters and teachers like Dr. Wayne Dyer, Esther & Jerry Hicks, Terry Small, Dr. Matthew James, Louise Hay, Marianne Williamson, Einstein, and others. It's also based on personal experience and first-hand knowledge of what works and what doesn't.

I believe in what I've learned and lived so strongly that I have received training and certification as a Certified Professional Coach and Neuro-Linguistic Programming (NLP) and Hypnotherapy Master Practitioner. I work with women every day who have used these keys and with fast results and incredible changes in their lives. I continue to personally use each and every one of these keys in my daily life. The changes you will achieve will depend on your own commitment and what you want to change in the first place.

I Am Handing You Proven Strategies That Will Help You Live the Life You Want!

Some of these strategies sound very simple, just like the key to empowering your own life. Yes, they *are* simple: so simple that you might want to dismiss them at first glance. Please don't. Changing your life doesn't have to be complicated or take a long time. What it does take is commitment from you to put yourself and your needs first, to work on yourself, to be honest and willing to make whatever changes you need to make to achieve the life you want.

You Must Be Willing To Let Go of Excuses

John Assaraf says when you're **interested,** *you do what's convenient; when you're* **committed,** *you do whatever it takes. These keys will light your path to your transformation into an empowered and fulfilled woman, a woman who has reclaimed herself and is now better able to not only fulfill her role as mom, wife, and professional, but also as a woman and a citizen of this world. You'll become a woman who knows that the world is a better place because she is living and walking this earth.*

Solution

You have the keys within yourself to unlock the door to endless possibilities. While some of these suggest actions, others are simply concepts that involve making a conscious choice. Practicing the actions will help you make them automatic.

It may seem uncomfortable in the beginning. You may even feel afraid to change. Remember what it was like learning to drive? It took patience and practice, didn't it? This will too, and that's okay. You've spent the last few decades of your life doing things a certain way, you won't unlearn those habits overnight. Cut yourself some slack and just keep going.

Fear is a normal response and it's not a bad thing unless it keeps you stuck. If you allow your ego to control your life, it will bring up a lot of fear. This is because the ego acts out of self-preservation. It likes the comfort zone you're in and wants to be in charge (even if it's not so comfortable, it is *familiar*). Be compassionate towards your ego. Work through the fear to move your life in the direction you want, rather than staying stuck where you don't want to be.

What Do You Do Next?

There are three requisites to creating change. First you must focus on what you want. Then you must clear out the negativity, limitations, and other mental and emotional gunk and sludge that is keeping you stuck. Third, you must maintain your focus and take action.

This book is divided into three sections. Begin by working through the first section on getting clear on what you want. Choose a key that you feel comfortable with and work on it for a one-week period. Once you master the key, choose another one. This process will take some time, and it is meant to . . . the purpose is not to overwhelm you. *I recommend first choosing the keys that speak to you the most or the ones that you know you can commit to easily.*

Commit to yourself 100% and don't waiver - no matter what anyone says. This is for you and you don't have to justify to anyone what you're doing or why. If you start to justify yourself, you will feel defensive and judged. This is about making *you* feel empowered and confident and clear about what you want and who you are.

Practice each key every day for a week and become consciously aware of how the key is working in your life. Notice the differences in how you think and feel. Practice and focus.

Once you have figured out what you want, you can move on to clearing out what's standing in your way. This time choose a key from section two and work on it for a week. Master that one and then pick the next one.

Once you have cleared out your "stuff," move on to section three and work on one key each week.

PART II

Keys For An Empowered Life

Section 1

Focus on What You Want

The Key of Doing What You Love

What are your goals? Why do you do the things you do every day? Is it because you **have to** or because you **want to**? Of course you have responsibilities . . . kids, home, career, spouse -- these are important and take up a lot of your time. Do you resent them because they are all you ever seem to do in your life?

Finding a goal that is meaningful to you changes your entire approach to achieving that goal. You are motivated and inspired to achieve it because you know it's part of your reason for being here. This doesn't mean you leave your life behind; it only means that you put more focus on what you love to do and reevaluate how and why you spend your time pursuing other activities and tasks.

Taking the time for a business or service you are passionate about, pursuing a hobby, your

21

favourite exercise or music recharges your batteries and brings joy. This lightens your burdens and your other tasks become more fulfilling. Because you are valuing yourself, you are building your self-esteem. Having something special that feeds soul lightens every other aspect of your day. Your life is not just about other people – it's about you too.

ACTION

Step 1. Identify what you love to do and explore the many ways to make time for these pursuits.

Step 2. Use the resources you have already or get the resources you need. With kids and their many activities and your other responsibilities, this may seem unrealistic, but there are some creative ways to find solutions. Perhaps there is child minding at the places where your activities take place. Or you hire a babysitter or trade babysitting roles with a friend. Maybe you can work on your passion before everyone wakens or when your children are tucked in bed. It may take some clever planning on your part, but it is worth the effort to know that you are taking care of your own needs as well.

Step 3. Notice how fulfilled and honored you feel now that you are doing these things for yourself.

Now capture your thoughts…what do you love to do?

The Key of Responsibility

Do you blame others for what goes wrong in your life? Do you feel like a victim? Understand that no one has the power to make you react to anything except you. That's right, you are the only one who can make that choice.

There are many expressions in the English language that shift responsibility from you to someone else. *"They* hurt my feelings." *"That* pisses me off." *"The economy* is bad." *The government* is..."

When you accept responsibility for your own responses to what occurs in your world, you stop victimizing yourself. This doesn't mean that you won't feel anger or sadness or happiness -- it just means that you have the power to change your reactions and how you want to feel as you go through life. Then the only one who can control you is *you*.

Being willing to change what's not working for you rather than denying responsibility makes you a more powerful person. Trying to get different results by doing and thinking the same things over and over just frustrates you.

ACTION

Step 1. Ask yourself: If there is a situation right now that you'd like to change, can you see how you might have played a role in the outcome?

Step 2. Being completely honest with yourself, work through these four questions with respect to the situation you identified. Notice how the emotion diffuses and how much more clarity you acquire about this situation.

- Is your current point of view or perspective helping you in this situation?
- Is the outcome of this situation something you can control or change?
- What could you do differently the next time you are in such a situation?
- What could you do to control or change your reaction in a similar situation to make things go more smoothly?

Now capture your thoughts…how will you take responsibility?

The Key of Awareness

The first step to any change is awareness. Once you are aware that you want to change something in your life, you can take the necessary steps to do it. The new path to achieve a new result may feel foreign to you in the beginning, so be patient with yourself.

It's important that whatever changes you want to make in your life you do because *you* want to make them, and not because someone else wants you to. Your awareness and desire for change -- along with your commitment to that change -- will help you make conscious choices with every step you take and every thought you have. It will become second nature to you to check and see if the choices feel good to you - and the choice will then be automatic.

ACTION

Step 1. Begin to notice the thoughts you have, the way you speak to yourself, the choices you make, the actions you take or don't take throughout the day.

Step 2. Become aware of how you feel in your body – does it feel good? Does it feel like a "yes?" Or do you get a sinking feeling or want to shrink down, rather than feeling joyful and expansive?

Step 3. Once you identify your patterns of what you accept and tolerate, you can use different tools to change them. Neuro-Linguistic Programming or

Hypnosis are fast working alternative therapies that create everlasting change fast.

Now capture your thoughts…how will you become more aware?

The Key of Rest

Once a week have a "Do Nothing" day. Yes, I know there is always something to be done. But constant action leads to burnout, frustration and resentment. You will be amazed at how recharged you will be for the remainder of the week if you allow yourself to have a day off from physical and mental work. It also helps if you can get away from your home or workspace for a "mini-vacation," even if it's a hike in the wilderness or a beauty treatment.

ACTION

Step 1. Consider what it would take for you to complete all the must-do responsibilities during six days of the week so that you could have one free day. This would be a day with no laundry, no cooking, no chores - only things you love doing. It may take some adjustments in your schedule and perhaps asking others to help you get things done or taxi the kids. It may mean you have to work harder during the rest of the week.

Step 2. Commit to yourself to have this Do Nothing Day every week.

Step 3. Remember if you don't get everything done during those six days, be kind to yourself and don't be tempted to squeeze them into your day off. This day is for you to completely relax, unwind and recharge, and spend quality time with yourself and your family.

Now capture your thoughts…how and when will you rest?

The Key of the Present

The only moment that you have complete control over is right now. What's in the past has already happened and you can't change that. You can think about the past and make choices about the future, but those thoughts and those choices are occurring in the now.

Do you label yourself as stressed? Stress is a thing that lives in the past and the future but not in the now. Think about it...what causes you stress? Stress is caused by an earlier event that you're still reacting to, and events that haven't happened yet that you're worried about.

Now think about this: Stewing about the past won't change it, and worrying about the future won't make it come faster or work out better.

ACTION

Step 1. Make the best choices you can about the future and learn from the past and stress won't affect you. There are many different ways to manage your stress and deal with your anxiety and help you uncover the learning you are meant to receive from a situation or event. These tools include NLP, Hypnosis, Exercise and others. Find the one that's best for you and do it. You will feel better and more balanced.

Step 2. As you go through your day, become aware of when your thoughts drift to the past or the future or when you're stumbling around "out of it" or spacey.

Step 3. Take your focus back to what you are doing and become fully present, give your work, your children or your husband your full attention and your life will become richer and filled with special moments. You will truly be *living* your life.

Now capture your thoughts…how will you stay present?

The Key of Emotion

Emotions are energies that vibrate at different frequencies. When we feel anger or happiness, we tend to attract other energy vibrating at the same level. Have you ever noticed that when you're having a great day, everyone seems to be smiling at you? You go with the flow, allowing everything to be smooth. When you're angry or sad, the world is bleak and wherever you turn you find more of the same.

When you find that you're feeling an emotion that you may label as negative such as frustration or sadness, allow yourself to feel the emotion rather than suppress it. Observe it. Don't judge it.

ACTION For Working With Negative Emotions

Step 1. Give yourself permission to feel the emotions you feel.

Step 2. Be safe about feeling the emotion – if you think that you will put yourself or another person in danger because of the emotion that you're feeling then remove yourself from the room. Go hit inanimate objects like pillows or blankets so that you don't hurt yourself. Go for a fast walk or run. Go clean the bathroom or fold laundry. The key is to let the emotion flow through you and release the energy in a non-threatening way.

Step 3. Realize that emotions are just energy that flows through us and once you understand that you are a channel for them and you are not defined by them, you will be able to observe them and then let them go and get back to yourself quickly.

Step 4. Get help releasing your negative emotions to clear up the past baggage you carry. There are many techniques you can use for releasing emotions such as hypnosis, Time Empowerment® Therapy, NLP, and others. Having worked with these techniques and I've seen how quickly and remarkably they work. You can learn more about them on my website: www.abundantmother.com.

ACTION   For Harnessing Your Passionate Emotions

Emotions can also be a wonderful guide for you if you're searching for your purpose or calling.

Step 1. Think about what it is that gets you really deeply emotional. What I'm describing here is not necessarily anything that makes you feel warm and fuzzy. Rather it's something that deeply moves you now and has in the past and you know it will continue to move you in the future.

If you think you're not living your calling, mission or purpose, then your emotions are the first place to look. They can tell you a lot about yourself. For example, do you really want to work with obese kids? Does the sight of an overweight child make you want to act and *do something*? Perhaps it's working with terminally ill patients or with animals?

Step 2. Avoid thinking about all the reasons why you can't do what your heart is calling you to do. Think about why you *can.*

Step 3. Take some time to envision yourself doing the work you desire. See the path that you have to take to get there. Remember, if you're committed, you do whatever it takes. This thing that gets you deeply emotional is very likely the calling you have on this planet and the purpose you are to serve. How long have you been ignoring it?

Step 4. Take the time to write out your visualization and the steps you will take to get there. This will make it real for you.

Step 5. Read this over every day to remind yourself and stay focused on your goal.

Step 6. Take action to move towards your goal – no matter how small the action is. Do something towards your goal at least 6 days a week.

Now capture your thoughts…how will you work through and harness your emotions?

The Key of Permission

Sometimes you just want to be angry or sad or you want to wallow in anger or sadness. In moments like these, no amount of convincing yourself will change the way you feel. Positive thoughts are very important, but when you're incapable of summoning a single positive thought, then you need to deal with the emotion you are feeling. Trying to suppress that emotion might make it go away for a time, but it won't be resolved.

We let our children cry when they are sad. We let them have their temper tantrums in their rooms when they can't cope with emotions they are experiencing. There is nothing wrong with allowing yourself to have a temper tantrum or a good cry as an adult. Sometimes things just get overwhelming and it's important to process that emotion and get the emotion out of your body so the energy can flow smoothly again instead of creating blockages or even dis-ease within you. Give yourself permission to have and experience your feelings so they can shift to a better emotion or a higher octave or vibration of feeling.

We talked about giving yourself permission. Giving permission to others includes letting them know what you find acceptable and what you don't, and this is done by setting boundaries. When we set boundaries, everyone knows what is expected of them. Clarity makes for smoother communication and cooperation. Setting boundaries with others at work, at home, and in all areas of your life is important.

There are some people who will not like the fact that you're making changes to spend time with yourself on what you love to do. Be okay with this. Give others the permission to have their own opinion, and to even leave your life if that's what must happen. Give yourself permission to be who you are meant to be.

Life has much to teach us and everyone must learn their own lessons. Sometimes this is painful to watch because we think we can help our friends or our children avoid a crushing experience and teach them the lesson ourselves. This is a compassionate thing to feel and want to do, however it may not be the best way for them to learn what they have to learn. Of course it's important for us to ensure that our children, friends, and family are safe, loved, and respected, but we also must step back and allow them their own experiences. If we prevent them from learning, they will likely come up against situations again and again that will bring them the same lessons over and over – perhaps in bigger and harsher ways.

ACTION

Step 1. When you are feeling engulfed in sadness or anger, permit yourself to experience the emotion.

Step 2. Feel it to whatever extent it needs to be felt. Make sure you and others are safe.

Step 3. Do any or all of the following actions:

- Cry.
- Punch a pillow (so you don't hurt your hand or someone else).
- Take a brisk walk or run.

- Do pages and pages of stream-of- consciousness writing about whatever is on your mind.
- Give yourself permission to be angry or sad for 10 or 15 minutes. Set a timer and when it rings ask yourself, "Am I finished wallowing?" No? Okay, then set the timer for another 5 or 10 or more minutes.

Step 4. Notice that these things will help you process your emotions and move on more easily. It may feel silly – so what! You will feel better and lighter quickly.

Step 5. Allow others to learn their own lessons. Keep your children safe and loved, yet refrain from sheltering or smothering them. The last thing you want is for your children to feel spoiled and entitled, so they refuse to take responsibility for their actions. Remember that they have a journey here that only they can take and lessons meant for them. Be mindful of the values and beliefs you are instilling in your children.

Step 6. Allow your friends and relatives to learn their own lessons. Be there for them, listen to them, but do not give them permission dump on you or wallow in the same story or drama over and over with no desire to change. Keep your own boundaries secure and don't take on their pain or problems as your own. Know that it is your right to your own feelings, and it is your right not to be a sounding board or emotional punching bag – you are to be loved and respected as a friend.

Now capture your thoughts…how will you give yourself permission?

The Key of Acknowledgement

Pat yourself on the back as often as you can. You are a fabulous and worthy human being just because you exist. You do the best you can with what you know and you have to give yourself a break sometimes. It's important to recognize not just the big accomplishments in your life, but also the little and medium ones too.

Think about it this way: how often do you berate yourself for little mistakes you make? You should be praising yourself just as often for all the small things that you do that are successful, thoughtful and brilliant. As your children grow up, when you teach them something like riding a bike, you give them lots of positive reinforcement, often repeatedly, for doing the same thing right. Even if they mess up, you tend to say it's okay and offer them encouragement to do it right the next time.

Just because you're an adult doesn't mean that you shouldn't receive positive reinforcement. You may tell yourself that since it's just expected of you to do things and do them right, why should you receive praise? How has this thinking worked for you so far? Remember you're working on empowering yourself and respecting yourself.

Paul Litwack, a master business coach and teacher says that 95% of people choose negative thoughts 95% of the time. That's a staggering number! Many people simply don't make the effort or just don't know that something as simple as giving yourself acknowledgment for a job well done is enough to start rewiring your neurology to

43

think more positive thoughts. Your brain can be rewired -- and if you consciously choose to positively acknowledge your small, medium, and large accomplishments, you will soon be hard-pressed to find a negative or berating comment flying through your head.

Brain cells (called neurons) can create new connections all throughout our lives. Information is passed from our brain throughout our body via chemicals called neurotransmitters. These chemicals are released by our brain according to our thoughts and emotions and are received in every cell in our body. When we think angry thoughts, the corresponding "angry" neurotransmitters flood our bloodstream and are accepted by receptor sites on our cells. The same thing happens when we think joyous, sad, loving and happy thoughts.

Research done by Dr. Deepak Chopra has demonstrated that our cells have the most receptor sites for the types of neurotransmitters they receive most often. Furthermore, when a cell dies, its replacement cell has twice as many receptor sites for that neurotransmitter. This means that if you're constantly bombarding yourself with negative thoughts and self-talk, your entire body gets so used to receiving the negativity, it stops recognizing positive things. Have you ever known anyone who is so unhappy or grumpy that they wouldn't know happiness if it hit them on the head?

The opposite is also true, and this is why you can rewire your neurology to be happier. There is a wonderful movie called "What The Bleep Do We Know" that explains this with incredible color graphics and animation. I recommend this movie to anyone who wants to understand how the mind works and can change for the better.

ACTION

Step 1. Become aware of everything you do throughout your day and tell yourself that you're doing a good job.

Step 2. Write down 3 to 5 things every evening that you did well that day. This may feel awkward at first if you're not used to receiving praise from yourself. You're learning a new behavior and it will take time to adopt it.

Step 3. Forgive yourself for small mistakes and let them go in the moment.

Step 4. When you catch yourself thinking a berating thought, make the effort to think the opposite. Instead of looking at all the things you think you do wrong, your brain will be wired to notice all the things you do well – and your accomplishments will multiply.

Step 5. Notice how this simple acknowledgment exercise lifts your confidence and respect for yourself. Your self-esteem and happiness quotient are skyrocketing.

Now capture your thoughts…how will you acknowledge yourself?

The Key of Honesty

It's good to come clean with yourself. You know yourself best, and only when you stop making excuses for yourself and to yourself will you begin to move forward.

Making excuses about why you can't or won't has gotten you to where you are today. When you want to create positive change, do you think that those excuses will serve you well? What has to change in order for you to live the life you want? What changes do you have to explore and make?

ACTION

Step 1. Be honest with yourself – always.

Step 2. When you find yourself going down the familiar road of making excuses as to why you can't or why you'll do something just this one last time – stop yourself and ask yourself if this choice will take you closer to your goal or further away.

Step 3. Ask yourself - do you mind taking a wrong turn on the way to your goal?

Step 4. If you do mind, then make the choice that will take you closer to your goal.

Now capture your thoughts…how will you be honest?

The Key of Excellence

Excellence is not perfectionism. It's been said that perfectionism is cause for procrastination. Truly, how can you ever finish something if you're waiting for it to be absolutely perfect? How do you feel about settling for excellence instead? In fact, take a look at any survey with a scale of experience...1 being poor and 5 (or 10) being excellent. It never says perfect.

You may label yourself as a perfectionist and that's your excuse for not starting a project or not finishing one. Ask yourself how is this label serving you and supporting what you want to accomplish in your life. Sell your perfectionism and purchase excellence and you'll be amazed at how different the world will be.

ACTION

Step 1. Make your own scale of experience so that you have descriptive words you are comfortable using instead of "perfect." Here are a few sample words you could incorporate into your scale of excellence:

All right / Not bad! / Okay / Good / Pretty good / Really good / Awesome / Great / Amazing / Excellent / Super.

Step 2. Every time you would normally use the word "perfect" substitute one of the other words that better describes what you actually think or feel about a situation or project.

Step 3. Understand that perfection is a fleeting state and puts you under a lot of pressure. Excellence or awesomeness or can be easily attained and are just as good.

Now capture your thoughts…how will you define your excellence?

The Key of Gratitude

Gratitude has the power to pull people out of depression. It is a perspective that allows you to be grounded in the present so you feel less stress. It lets your brain release endorphins that bring on feelings of happiness and well-being.

Every moment of every day you have a choice to make. You can be happy and grateful or you can be miserable and angry. Only you have the power to make that choice. By choosing gratitude for everything in your life, you're able to focus on what's important.

Sure it's nice to have your "stuff" and a fulfilling job and all those other things that you think will make you happy. But if all of that was taken away and all you had was *you* . . . how would you choose to be then?

You are not what you have. You are not what you do. You are not what others think of you. You are worthy and amazing just because you are -- and gratitude reinforces this.

ACTION

Step 1. Take the time to think about what you are grateful for in your life, in your day-to-day existence, and in this moment.

Step 2. Take the time each day to write several things that you are grateful for. If you can only think of one, that is excellent. These can be as simple or as elaborate as you like: your children or your favourite tea mug. Some days you may have more things to be grateful for than others – this is fine! *It's important to begin noticing the people and things around you that bring you joy and energy.*

Step 3. You can make a gratitude board where you list the things you are grateful for and look at it often.

Step 4. You can play the gratitude game with your children or spouse when you're in the car or at the table. Take turns telling the other players what you love about each of them and about yourself.

Now capture your thoughts…how will you express your gratitude?

Section 2

Clearing out the Mental, Emotional and Spiritual Gunk and Sludge

The Key of Letting Go

You probably like to do things your way because no one else can do it as well as you can, right? While this may be true with some tasks, I'm willing to bet it's not always the case. There are many ways of accomplishing something and no one way is perfect.

Think about how much advice you get about raising kids, gardening or running your household. It's all different and much of it comes from people who have a little or a lot of success and experience in the areas they are advising you on. This means that even though they do it differently than you do, it still works out in the end.

ACTION

Step 1. When you find yourself overwhelmed with everything, it's a good idea to think about where you could let go and what you would be comfortable delegating.

Step 2. *Ask for help when you need it and let someone else do it. Ask your friends, your family or hire someone, depending on what you've decided to delegate -- even if you don't think they'll do it*

55

right. Consider if their way is really wrong or is it just different and your ego is getting in the way?

Step 3. Practice letting go and just taking your ego out of it so that you can focus on something you love to do or more important issues, while others are taking care of the tasks you've delegated.

Now capture your thoughts…how will you let go more?

The Key of Forgiveness

Ever notice how children don't hold grudges? They may get upset and even have spectacular meltdowns, but they get over it and go on to the next exciting toy, book or game. As adults we forget how to let the past go. We think about it, stew about it, worry about it, and often expect it to repeat itself in the future.

You would feel lighter if you learned from your past and then just let it go, wouldn't you? This is the only thing you can really do -- because you can't change the past, you can only change your view of it.

Forgiving someone does not mean you condone what they did or said. It does not mean that you want to reconcile with them. It does not mean that you won't pursue justice if necessary.

What it does mean is that you've chosen to move forward with *your* life and to stop being the victim of the event. You have reclaimed your power back from the person who wronged you and they can no longer make you feel bad, angry, sad, or anything else.

It is important to forgive yourself too. We've all done things we're not proud of and may regret. Did you learn something from what you did? Take what you learned and move on. There is no point in holding a grudge against yourself and letting it limit you from reaching your ultimate dreams. I'm a firm believer that everything happens for a reason. We all do the best we can with what we know and the resources we have. If you look at your past from that perspective, then it will be easier for you to live in the present and let the past stay in the past where it belongs.

ACTION

Forgiveness is very individual but there are many ways to facilitate the process for yourself. Here are some suggestions

Step 1. Writing about the incident. You can write in a private forgiveness journal you can write a letter to the person or to yourself and bury it or burn it; you don't have to send it. You can also write out a conversation with the person or with yourself during which you talk about forgiveness and what has to happen in order for you to be able to forgive.

Step 2. You can also utilize visualization to facilitate this process for yourself. Below is an example of a visualization. The Hawaiian Ho'oponopono forgiveness process is a simple visualization process that you can use to forgive.

1. Imagine you are sitting on a stage and you have another stage in front of you.
2. Above your head is a source of healing light. Allow it to envelop your whole being and heal you from the inside out.
3. Bring out onto the stage the people you will forgive, either one at a time or in groups. Allow the healing light to come out of your heart and heal them too.
4. Say whatever you need to say to them and have them say to you whatever you would imagine they would need to say.

5. Tell them "I forgive you, please forgive me too" until you know that forgiveness has happened. Remember this is all in your mind, the other person doesn't have to know about you having done this process in order for the forgiveness to take place.

6. Imagine the cord of energy that connects you with the person(s) on stage and gather them all up. Imagine cutting these cords with a sharp beam of light from above your head. To reconnect with fresh energy all you have to do is think of the person in their new, cleaned-off fresh state.

7. Imagine a golden source of energy above your head that's filled with all of your own unique life force essence in it and then have it come down and fill you with it. This essence and life force stays with you always. Allow the stages to dissolve after you've completed the forgiveness process.

Now capture your thoughts…who do you want to forgive and when?

The Key of Language

Words have the power to evoke powerful emotion. They can move you to laughter and happiness or to anger and tears. The words you say to yourself have a lot to do with your state of mind and the current direction of your life.

Many women struggle with negative self talk. Since the unconscious mind (also called the subconscious mind) does not distinguish between what's real and what's perceived, when you talk negatively to yourself, you give your mind powerful suggestions that that's how you really are. Do you want to continue to believe that you're lost, frustrated, stupid, and whatever else you tell yourself?

In addition, words like "should," "must" and "have to" can make you feel guilty if you don't follow through on what you should, must, or have to do. You are an amazing person and worthy of respect and love. You are working on moving your life forward in the direction you choose, and making yourself feel guilty will hinder your progress. Words that bring on guilt and shame bring with them heaviness and frustration. It's important to consider the language you are using not only with others, but with yourself too.

ACTION

Step1: Begin to notice the stream of thoughts running through your head. They go fast, so it will take you time to learn to listen to them.

Step 2: Write them down. What types of words do you predominantly hear yourself using?

Step 3: Think about how these words make you feel and how you would like to feel instead. Ask yourself: Are they true? When did you decide to start using these words with yourself?

Step 4: What types of words could you use instead to make yourself feel loved, balanced, refreshed, respected?

Step 5: When you catch yourself saying negative things to yourself choose positive words instead.

Now capture your thoughts…what language do you use with yourself?

The Key of Self Care (Good Health)

Your healthy body is like a car with a full tank of gas. When your car is low on fuel, you stop and refuel it. Your body needs the same type of attention. It uses food for energy and exercise for maintenance. By feeding your body poorly and not exercising, you run the risk of attracting dis-ease. Although it is not the intention of this report to teach you about nutrition and exercise, your health is an important factor in your overall wellbeing. When you are in poor health, it is difficult to focus on other aspects of you life. Research has shown, too, that some types of dis-ease manifest because of bottled-up emotions and unresolved past issues.

ACTION

It is imperative to take good care of your body. Seek the help of your doctor, a personal trainer, nutritionist, or other alternative therapy practitioners if you don't know where to start.

Now capture your thoughts...how will you take care of yourself?

Section 3

Goal Setting, Maintaining Focus and Taking Action

The Key of Goal Setting

Knowing exactly what you want and making sure that this goal is aligned with your values is a crucial first step in making it happen. Although it's fun to be spontaneous and carefree about certain things in life, it's also important to have short and long-term plans for how you will get to where you want to go in life.

ACTION

Step 1: Once you've established the direction that you want to take in your life, write down your goals. Writing them down makes them more tangible for you.

Step 2: Use the SMART acronym when writing your goals. It's a great way to set yourself up for success. Here are the steps:

1) Be **Specific**- Write the goal in a way that is very detailed. Answer the questions of who is involved, what do you want to accomplish, where, by when, why – is this goal only for you?
2) Make it **Measurable** - how will you know when you accomplish it?

3) Make it **Attainable** – does this goal stretch your abilities? What resources do you already have? What do you need to learn or get to achieve it?
4) Be **Realistic** – is this a goal that you are willing and able to work for? Is this only for you? Will the other people involved slow this down?
5) **Time Bound** – by when do you want to accomplish this goal?

Step 3: Read your goals once in the morning after you wake up and once just before you go to bed. This will help you remain focused. You can write them on index cards for easy handling.

Now capture your thoughts...what are your goals?

The Key of Taking Action

Positive thoughts alone won't get you all the way there. The key to accomplishing anything is actually *doing* it. Once you figure out what changes you want to make in your life and you write the plan to achieve those changes, you have to take a deep breath and just go for it.

You will feel fear – sure you will. This is all new to you. Even when you've mastered all of these keys you will feel fear. It's a natural emotion that we humans feel. What will change with time is your reaction to fear. You will know that a particular fear is like radar for you. If you're afraid of taking a step, then perhaps you need to weigh all your options and make sure you've made the best possible choice. After that, you feel the fear and go for it. Focus on the positive outcomes of your actions and let the positive vibrations of those thoughts bring into your life what you desire. All successful people feel the fear - it's human. They choose to act in spite of it.

ACTION

Step 1: Write down your plan.

Step 2: Ask yourself and contemplate these questions. You can write out your answers if you want:
- What's the absolute worst that can happen?
- What's the best-case scenario?
- What do you want to happen?
- Is it within your control to make the best-case scenario happen?

- How will you do that?
- What resources do you have that will help you?
- What do you still need to learn?

Step 3: Remember that what you think about expands. If you don't know how to tackle a big task, then break it down into smaller steps and take action!

You can't mow a lawn in your mind...eventually you will have to go out and mow.

Now capture your thoughts…what actions will you take and when?

The Key of List Making

To clear your mind: Lists are simple and can be wonderful tools that you can use to help yourself not only get organized but also purge your mind of things that are taking up space. Lists also help break down a seemingly overwhelming task into manageable steps.

It's important to realize that you don't have to do everything on your list if you don't want to. This exercise is more for storing information accurately for yourself so that you can be mindful with whatever is at hand, like your child wanting to read a book or do a puzzle.

The point of lists is not to bog yourself down with a whole bunch of things to do, but to be confident that if you need to remember something, it will be right there for you to read. You can use a scrap paper or have a book or journal for your list. Use whatever is easy and convenient for you.

ACTION

Step 1: Make lists of everything that's on your mind- whether it's groceries, things you have to do or don't want to do, events you have to attend, or other activities that distract you from being in the present moment. Lists are powerful because they ease your mind from having to remember everything. By writing things down and putting the list in a safe space you don't have to worry about forgetting something – it's on your trusty list!

To Get Organized: Lists are also useful to break down a project or task that seems insurmountable or one that you're procrastinating on. If you write down every single step that you need to do from beginning to end and then just start at step one, the task will not be so gigantic in your mind. It will be like walking on pebbles instead of climbing a mountain. You'll just be taking a bunch of little steps towards your goal and crossing them off your list as you go. Trust me; there is nothing as satisfying as crossing things off a list with a red or black felt-tip pen. If you need a pick-me-up, make a list of all the things you've accomplished in a day and then just cross them off. It will show you just how much you have to be proud of and doing and it will make you laugh. Instant gratification!

ACTION

Step 1: Write your big goal on the top of a page.

Step 2: Write down every step you can think of that needs to be done to accomplish the goal, whether you have the resources or knowhow or not – those will become clear later.

Step 3: Remain focused on the end goal you want and take action, then cross off each step as you accomplish it.

Now capture your thoughts...how can you use lists to help you?

The Key of Flexibility

Sometimes the best-laid plans don't work exactly the way you wanted. There could be many reasons for this. What's your automatic reaction when something goes awry? Remember that what you focus on is what you attract into your life. Rather than thinking about the difficulties that these changes present, what could you focus on instead? What could you do to adjust the plan to make it work? *The opportunities that arise out of new situations can lead to a new path that you hadn't considered before.*

ACTION

Step 1: Seek out the opportunities or lessons that present themselves when something doesn't go your way.

Step 2: Make whatever necessary corrections need to be made and get right back into action. Have the flexibility to consider new options and other possibilities out there.

Step 3: Come at a problem with a creative mindset rather than an angry or resentful mindset and notice how empowered you are to solve it more easily.

Step 4: Brainstorm or mind-map ideas and before you know it a solution will be right in front of you.

Step 5: Take action every day towards what you want.

Now capture your thoughts…how will you be more flexible?

The Key of Positive Thought

Thoughts are energies that vibrate at different frequencies. Positive thoughts vibrate higher than negative thoughts. What has been discovered about the human mind is that at the unconscious level it doesn't differentiate between what is real and what is perceived. The unconscious part of our mind mind also does not process negatives.

If I said to you, "Don't think of a blue tree," what immediately pops into your mind? A blue tree! The very thing that you were trying not to think about. This means that you can't not think about something without first thinking about it.

This really is simple: when you say to yourself "I don't want to be tired," your unconscious mind hears "I want to be tired" and it helps you feel more tired. If you say to yourself "I don't want to be broke," your unconscious mind hears "I want to be broke" and supports you in what you want.

Therefore, in order to really get what you want you have to say it how you want it. For example "I want to feel vibrant and awake all the time" or "I want to be financially secure." This positive type of thinking and self talk keeps you and your unconscious mind focused on what you want.

Thanks to research done on the power of the mind by Dr Deepak Chopra and his colleagues, we have a better understanding of how we can consciously direct our lives. *What types of thoughts do you want to think if you want to change the direction of your life? You know that thoughts are also tied to feelings and emotions, and if emotions act like magnets that attract more of the same, then what types of thoughts will you choose to think?*

ACTION

Step 1: Give yourself permission to make mistakes and to change. Changing your thinking will feel awkward at first if you are used to hearing the negative stream of thoughts in your mind.

Step 2: Listen to your thoughts and write the negative ones down. It will take practice to choose different thoughts.

Step 3: Challenge the negative thoughts and realize they are not true. They are based on decisions you've made about yourself in the past that are not based on fact. It's important to become aware of the thoughts you are having and to choose ones that are aligned with your new path. What would you rather believe and think about yourself instead? You can also consult techniques like NLP that speed up this process.

Now capture your thoughts...how will you guide your own thoughts?

The Key of Celebration

When you hear the word "celebration," you probably think of milestones like birthdays or anniversaries or special occasions like graduations or holidays. These are all great reasons to celebrate.

What about the small achievements and goals you reach in your daily life? Things like being half or two-thirds finished with a project? Or even finally finishing something that you've been putting off – like ironing? It's important to celebrate these too. This doesn't mean you have to have a party with balloons and cake. There are other ways to celebrate goal achievements.

It's good to celebrate reaching your goals and finishing projects and tasks because it gives you a sense of accomplishment. It doesn't make you feel like you're constantly running after a carrot on a stick and never accomplishing anything.

This does not mean you don't make new goals and set new tasks. It's more about being grateful and happy with what you have accomplished. This empowers you and gives you the energy to accomplish even more exciting goals.

ACTION

Step 1: Think about the ways that you can celebrate the small and medium goals and tasks that you finish or are close to finishing. What makes you feel encouraged and happy? This can be something simple like visiting a favourite bookstore or coffee

81

shop, taking a walk or favorite hike in nature, or buying yourself something luxurious.

Step 2: Write a list of these activities or items and have it readily available and choose one every time you reach 90% of a goal or finish a task. Notice how fun it is to make the list – and how fun it is to do something to celebrate *yourself*.

Now capture your thoughts…what, how, and when will you celebrate?

***

If you follow these steps mindfully, you'll be on your way to self-mastery, knowing the way to want to feel in every moment, and creating your life one consciously aware moment at a time. You'll sail through less desirable tasks because of your positive mindset and increased energy. You'll find that you'll begin to love your life. Positive opportunities will be offered to you effortlessly because you put in the time, commitment and positive intention to change your life. For those of you who have taken this challenge, know that you are making a huge difference. I offer you my gratitude and I salute your courage, commitment and self-love!

Sources and Recommended Further Reading

Chopra, D. (1990) Quantum Healing: Exploring the Frontier of Mind/Body Medicine. Bantam Books.

Chopra, D. (1994) Seven Spiritual Laws Of Success. San Rafael CA: Amber Allen Publishing

Dyer, W. (2004) The Power Of Intention: Learning to Co-Create Your World Your Way. Hay House Inc.

James, M. (2010) The Foundation of Huna: Ancient Wisdom For Modern Times. Kailua-Kona HI: American Pacific University Press.

Lipton, B. (2008) The Biology Of Belief: Unleashing the Power of Consciousness, Matter & Miracles. Hay House Inc.

Talbot, M. (1991) Holographic Universe. Harper Collins.

85

About the Author

Kasia Rachfall's passion and mission is to empower and inspire parents and kids from the inside out.

As a business owner, speaker and working mother, Kasia knows what it takes to cope with the realities of everyday life. Family, career, and relationships can cause us to put ourselves at the bottom of our priority list – causing the whole family dynamic and meaningful communication to suffer.

Kasia brings extensive expertise and passion in personal growth and development. She is devoted to enabling parents to successfully identify and release the lies they tell themselves that brought them to the frustrating place they may find themselves in.

Specializing in Neuro-Linguistic Programming, Hypnosis, and Time Empowerment® Therapy, Kasia guides parents to quickly release what's holding them back and break through their mental and emotional barriers to be strong, confident and raise responsible, authentic, self assured children.

Kasia received her Bachelor of Business Administration (BBA) from Simon Fraser University in Burnaby, BC, where she focused on communication and marketing. She holds the International Coach Federation (ICF) accredited

Certified Professional Coach designation from International Coach Academy, NYC. Kasia is also an Accredited Trainer and Master Practitioner of Neuro-Linguistic Programming (NLP), Hypnosis and Time Empowerment® Therapy through The Empowerment Partnership, a division of Kona University, HI. She was trained by Dr Matthew B. James, one of the most sought after NLP Masters in the industry who studied with Richard Bandler, a founding father of NLP. Kasia also holds a Masters Degree in Transpersonal Psychology at Kona University.

She lives in the Vancouver, BC, area with her husband and kids. Visit her online at www.abundantmother.com.

www.ingramcontent.com/pod-product-compliance
Lightning Source LLC
Chambersburg PA
CBHW060402050426
42449CB00009B/1861